FIRST PUBLISHED
JANUARY, 1938
1000 COPIES

RACINE

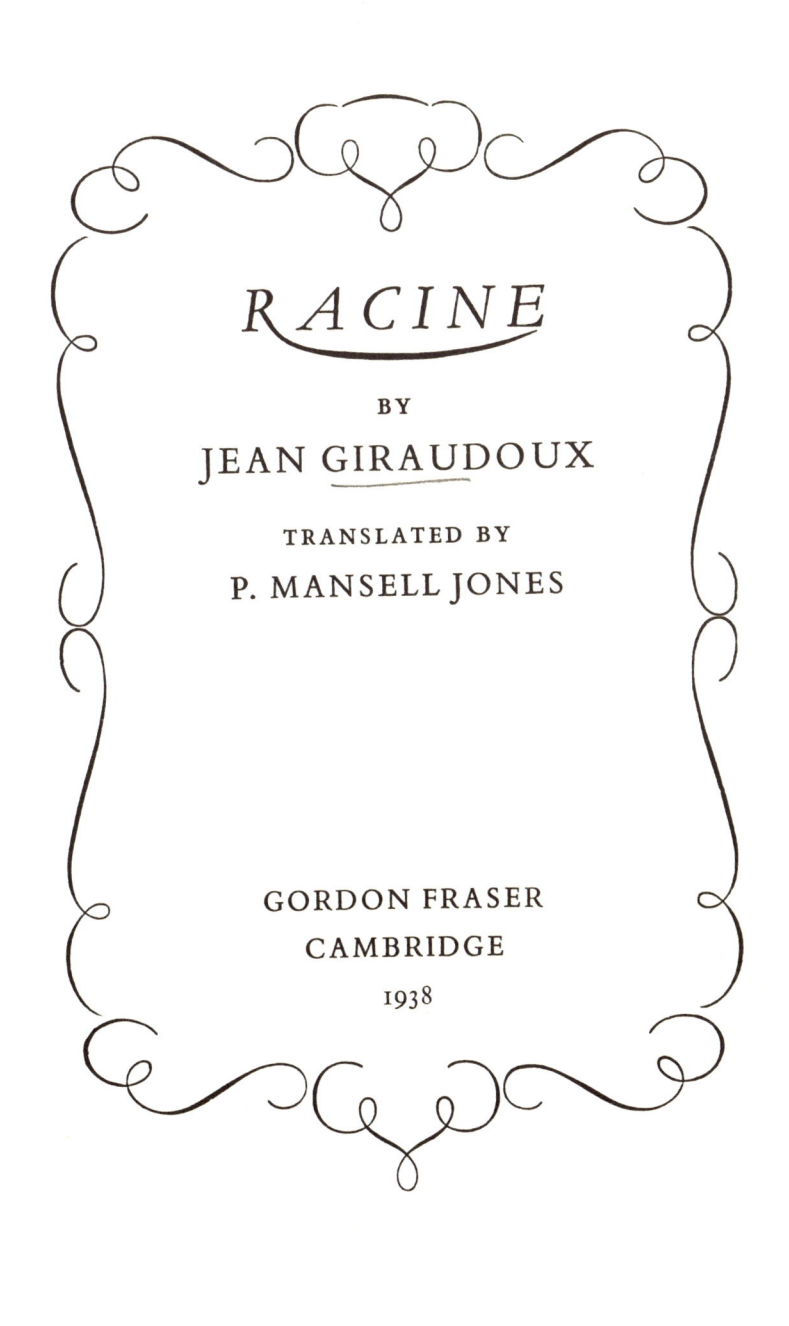

BY
JEAN GIRAUDOUX

TRANSLATED BY
P. MANSELL JONES

GORDON FRASER
CAMBRIDGE
1938

PRINTED IN GREAT BRITAIN

RACINE

It is satisfying to think that the foremost writer in the literature of France is not a moralist or a scholar or a general or even a king, but a man of letters. Those who still believe in genius have for their part in contemplating Racine an opportunity to notice that in a civilisation where all the summits are attained and each of whose members receives a soul equally nurtured in all its parts, genius has no claim to stake against talent. It is such a civilisation itself—whether it be of Pericles or of Louis XIV—which is the genius; a civilisation which by the very fact of its density frees the soul from those vacuities and viscosities through which are obtained perhaps more dramatic or more mysterious, but always to some extent deceptive, illuminations; a civilisation which rears the man of letters in a stately tranquillity, raising him above histrionics and confession, and making him responsible for an ultimately perfect acoustic. The virtue of a successful civilisation is such that in place of the restricted means by which, in unfinished epochs, writers acquire experience—misfortunes, the observation of men, crises cardiac or conjugal—is substituted in those happier periods a congenital knowledge of great hearts and great moments. Racine is the finest illustration of this truth. No childhood was further removed than his from the laws and adventures of childhood; not only is he deprived of his father and mother, but in view of the singular and vehement personages who surround him, it is astonishing that one of them could be found to teach him to walk. His adolescence is no less theoretical; to protect him from the world a ring of aged Jansenists hedges in the flowery lawn where the young Racine devotes himself, between visits from ladies and gentlemen who are strictly Greeks and Romans, to occupations which are as passionate as they are imaginary. Study and the joy of studying supplant in his case all contact with life, all happiness and disaster, until the day when he enters a world still more devoid of foundation than the one in which he has lived so far, the world of the theatre. All told he knows only operations of the mind and people in fancy dress. But, and let us not deny this apotheosis to the art of writing, it happens that from this contact between youth which had never been young and a milieu of artifices, there suddenly comes to birth the most direct and realistic work of the century. The laws of aesthetics are doubtless as rigid as the laws of mathematics; his discoveries about men Racine arrives at with an indifference, a detachment from humanity as great as that which the geometrician has from the daily life and family routine of figures and forms. There is not a sentiment in

Racine which is not a literary sentiment. Handsome, sensible and elegant, he passes the recruiting board for great men of letters brilliantly, along with Sophocles and Goethe; in neither body nor mind does he conceal one of those imperfections or peculiarities which make the work more personal and more human. Nothing in him is visionary or real or frenzied or despondent. His bitterness, when he is bitter, does not come from the fact that he is deceived or that he limps; or his mildness from the fact that he is at peace, or his vigour from his being Herculean—but from his being a writer. His method, his only method, consists in taking from without in a net of style and poetics a catch of truths of which he himself suspects nothing but that they are there, and in utilising to the extreme limit the potentialities that a culture and a language naturally possess to mould moral realities under the caress of talent. Even the motive force behind this talent is purely literary. Of all the great questions which the movement of thought or which circumstance or simply fashion raises during his time, and which leave their mark even in the letters of Mme de Sévigné—not only is Racine never inspired, he has not allowed one of these things to penetrate his inner life.

But were there no crises and excitements in his religion? Although he lived in the very centre of the quarrels, never does he examine himself, I won't say about God, but on a question of dogma. The replies he made to the attacks of the world, the cries he raised in affliction were not professions of faith but epigrams and distiches. As is natural with so ardent and susceptible a spirit, satire alone is what the adventures of life inspire in him. The only piece dictated to him by experience is *Les Plaideurs*, and no one would say it is the sort of play we call Racine. His most violent reactions were not provoked by religion but by sectarians. He had with the Jansenists the kind of dispute the choir-boy has with the deacons: Pascal had his with God. To Racine, to the life of Racine, the bourgeois parables of the Bible, the Prodigal Son and the rest, are easily applicable as they are to the acts of every member of the Christian flock, that is to every common Christian: the parables perish in the light of Pascal's countenance. Racine's spell of dissipation was never a phase of impiety: he is reconciled not with God but with his aunt; he orders his grave not at the feet of a saint, but at the feet of the man who taught him Greek roots. In that fine but fatal enterprise which, in a century marked by terrible extremes of personal liberty, the Jansenists undertook at that Port-Royal of theirs (named like the harbour in the Indies raided by a band of corsairs or outlaws), Racine never took part, having fled like a cabin-boy on arriving at the first place of call, to join the boat again when it had become a pontoon. He did not know or even suspect anything of the venture. He separated from the Jansenists—quite naturally—when he saw his family in them, and he came back to them no less naturally when he saw them as friends. Those who know God are aware that the word Friendship is the feeblest of expressions for rallying people to the faith, and can only serve the timid and ignorant who are incapable of uttering the all-important passwords. The relations that people would like to find between his heroes, his heroines and an original religious conviction have likewise no existence. The alleged Jansenism of *Phèdre*, if we must refer to it as such, yields in vigour and conviction to the Jansenism of the heroes of Aeschylus; and moreover, never since the birth of tragedy has tragic action consisted of anything but the projection of fatality upon a chosen being. The two Catholic pieces, *Esther* and *Athalie*, are explained by the Catholicism of Louis XIV and not by that of the author. Besides, they are not Catholic but Hebrew, and never did Racine come nearer to the truth of antiquity—biblical in this case—than in the description of the grandeur and realism of the Jews, of which perhaps he never knew a specimen. During his whole dramatic career the religious life of Racine shrinks to that vague unconscious type of Christianity, common enough by the way with the French, the deposits of which act like a vaccine but never like a ferment.

And what of the worldly part of his life, his dissipations and adventures? It has no more vivid peculiarity to show. The reasons for it and the circumstances in which it develops never raise Racine above the most habitual human acts. None of his gestures or his tastes ever carries him beyond the kind of culture doled out to the choir-boys of literature. Never does he graze the magnetic danger points of human knowledge. The shudder of a young soul approaching the heart of a mystery was never felt by Racine. One looks in vain in his first essays for the equivalent of those studies of Pascal on the void, which were essays in the approach to nothingness. Geometrical figures, metaphysics, thought repel him; he is too fond of a sustained style for the punctuated brevities of the world to interest him. Deprived of parents, weaned when quite young from family instincts, he overflows in affection for a conventionalised nature, a literary world of which he is the young and chaste satyr. Absorbed in flooding the walls and valleys of Jansenism with the sunlight of Theocritus, he tastes romance in the least noxious doses. His retreat within the sacred precincts has made him not a Levite but a provincial, while the only ambitions he has are those of a man of letters whom Paris attracts. His desire is to get published, he likes writing articles, he seeks correspondents, he would have invented the gazette. When he goes for a spell into the provinces themselves, he does not enjoy their charm otherwise than do Chapelle and Bachaumont; and in none of his verses do the landscape and climate of Uzès make themselves felt, whereas the least dip, the least ripple associated with the regions of Tragedy is immediately recorded. If on his return to Paris, his life becomes irregular, this is not due to any originality of character or to exigencies of personal temperament, but to the very defects or qualities of the born *littérateur*. What is called his period of dissipation consists only of distractions of a professional order, that is the contrary of those into which inspired minds generally fall. If there is a love affair it is with a comedienne. If there are affairs of honour, they are occasioned by his tragedies. Never has an author clung so nervously to the success of his plays or defended masterpieces more by insisting on their inferior sides and his own. Here we find nothing of those trances by means of which Chateaubriand or Vigny made their pregnancy seem divine, claimed on its behalf a significance for contemporary humanity, increased their present by their posthumous fame and ended by appearing less the fathers than the sons of their works and labours. For Racine the birth of a tragedy is first a question of subject, then of composition, then of development. When the word "death" comes under his pen, he does not think of his own death. No more than of his shadow when he writes the word "shadow" or of his mistress when he writes the word "mistress" or of La Champmeslé when he writes Hermione....He composed the dream of Athalie, and yet he could dream himself.... He simply feels the ease with which his talent works and the responsibility of seeing himself become the appointed purveyor to his country and his king. As chamberlain of the tragic flock, he always chose his heroines by their titles to nobility or beauty, before knowing what they were going to personify. Andromaque, Monime, Phèdre were first engaged on the strength of their appearance and complexion, and *en bloc*, as dancers. Roles so perfect, so apt to utilise to the extreme the qualities of actresses and actors, can only have been created by the craftsman's instinct and not by the hazard of inspiration. Hence, moreover, as a counter-effect of his craft, dominating his tragedies as a potter his vases, Racine regains at an incomparably higher level the role of creator which other dramatists surrender in their struggle with, or their indulgence for, their work. But that is also why literary explanations and commentaries are the only ones which permit of approach to the poet, the only ones to which he would willingly have listened—this poet for whom one could have engraved the following epitaph: Here lies he who never set himself the problem of God or of knowledge or of the minds of animals, he for whom problems of politics, rank and morality had no existence: Here lies Racine.

The question of the theatre was not even raised at the time when Racine began to write. A stage and a public were at his disposal from the start. It would have been regrettable for him to have had to lose time in reforming or innovating. The theatre is a microcosm which should display, at their highest pitch of colour and passion, the tendencies, potentialities and accomplishments, poetical, moral and sensuous, of an epoch. But it cannot create organs of reception in the spectator;

these it presupposes. A century or an epoch of literary greatness may terminate with an important period for the theatre, but the latter never comes first. Good drama is a lavish appropriation of elements that are perfect: while a reader may look for revelations in what he reads, all that a playgoer wants is to enjoy the spectacle before him. This excludes from the true stage every manifestation which is simply an investigation or a lesson and which cannot instinctively wed the life of drama as a contemporary creation; such a manifestation may lack that lustre an epoch derives from courtiers in court-dress or from the latest searchlights, or again that modern type of acting perfected by gymnastics and phonetics, or lastly the style and the *motifs* of a type of poetry, fiction or music which is fully adult. Great drama is that which convinces minds already convinced, moves souls already stirred, dazzles eyes already lit, and which at the end leaves the spectators with the impression of a proof, the proof of their own sensibility and their own epoch. It is as a pupil submissive to the fashion and laws of the genre that Racine enters the stage. He comes to it as Louis XIV does, and luckily at the same time. With the young king the excitement of absolute power, the admiration of an incomparable assembly were bound to raise court life to the highest pitch that the pomp and religion of royalty are capable of attaining—to spectacular display. With the young writer the effervescence and vanity of poetry led inevitably to the adoption of the only genre which adequately separates the author from the mass of humanity, that is to dramatic art. Experience had shown him that one elegiac writer is related to all the others by a network of communications; that he is caught in a wave of sensibility which is hardly original at all; and that it is the most lonely of elegists who, contrary to appearances, gives himself up to the most public of literary operations. Lyricism and effusion are really like sports in public baths. But the dramatic poet isolates himself sternly from the crowd, not merely from his colleagues in emotional excitement, but from those thousands of spectators whose single brow leans against the stage more heavily than a battering-ram; and young Racine, anxious at once for personal cleanliness and for success, was to turn rapidly to that personification of himself which for another ten years would preserve him from life. He throws himself into it. He no more dreams of perfecting the organs of the theatre than does an assassin of improving on the dagger which honest cutlers have forged for him. The assassin is out for blood, so is young Racine. All those improbable precautions applied to works based on fables in order to make them probable are natural to him. He never indulges in an innovation, a technicality or a formula which is new. He accepts the rules of the game. He readily abandons a whole section of the heroes of his imagination, Théogène, Chariclée, probably Daphnis and probably Chloe—all those that would have led him to a genre in which poetic relativity, the artificial liberty of the feelings would have had too big a share—towards tragi-comedy about which he had been thinking for a moment. What would he have made of a dying genre, dying, too, in an atmosphere of smiles and graces? If tragi-comedy split up of a sudden into tragedy and comedy, it was not only because Aristotle was winning, nor because it was definitely necessary from motives of literary hygiene to separate heroes destined to die from heroes destined to marry. The reason was the same which, in centuries that are great centuries, transforms idyllic poets into poets laureate, and preachers of picturesque sermons into great orators. It was because of an endeavour common to all great optimistic and constructive periods, which consists in banishing, in solemn assemblies, for as many minutes and as remotely as possible, all traces of laughter from the human face. Centuries of perfect civilisation imply of necessity those assemblies in which, each night, faces which by day had worn a witty or a sneering expression are smoothed and purified by a severe and tragic spectacle. The Anglo-Saxon's two minutes' silence marks a strictly measured piety as against those three hours of anguish. Not a laugh, not a smile will be found in the work of Racine. Never has the mask of the human face been more carefully respected, more rigidly fixed. The work of Racine is indeed the high mass of that human and worldly century, filling for the age of Louis XIV the same symbolic role as the *danse macabre* filled for the age of the Capets. One sees at once what quarterings of nobility death had acquired in the interval.

On this stage which has become a kind of altar, Racine can without difficulty become the poet who has brought tragedy nearest to human sacrifice. That cannibalism which the Greeks reserved in their attitude to gods, demi-gods and heroes, which was subsequently maintained up to the Renaissance in the form of the Passion, and to which after Jodelle, all French tragedians, falling upon their plumed victims, abandoned themselves—it is Racine who makes all this real and who compounds his heroes of elements which are the nearest to true flesh and blood. It may surprise us that he went to antiquity to choose such living victims. Contrary to what may be believed, when Racine began, plays of a European type with almost modern characters were the fashion. From Corneille to Rotrou, from Prévost to Borée, all tragic poets were bent precisely on withdrawing from the classical atmosphere and giving France a rejuvenated and European mythology. To this Racine paid no attention. For it he would have had to change his universe. He would have had to kill heroes who had not been his lifelong friends, sacrifice women with whom his childhood had not been spent; in short he would not have had himself to submit to martyrdom and to those torments of family affliction which still make us connect Racine's face with the visage of each of his heroines. For it is with them he had his real liaisons and from the time he began to read; his terrific sense of experience he got not from bourgeois love affairs with an honest actress, but from the passionate life he led, between twelve and twenty, with the complicity of tutors who later on could not really reproach him with Phèdre, since it was they themselves who had given her to him as playmate and fellow-communicant.

They had evidently not realised the danger and were merely following methods which had been erroneous for centuries. It was indeed the religious education which had created, collaterally, the classical and pagan education. It was popes and monks, the members of the strictest orders, who had founded and legitimatised for young Racine's good, alongside the Christian world all of whose heroes had no alternative but to be Christians, a world whose heroes were profane. It happened that, differing in this from all other religions, Mussulman, Buddhist, Jewish or the rest, the Christian religion admitted to a place near the pious conception of the soul, a soul of the imagination with martyrs, saints and demons of the imagination. By a premeditated decision, strange in appearance, the future defender of God and Jansenius, after prayers and the sacred history lesson, would suddenly enter a universe of human sacrifice, incest and adultery, where he moved about freely under the eyes of his masters. It was even allowed that these unreal beings and events had left traces on earth. Corresponding to all these inventions of the mind were memorials and countries: before the tomb of that Pylades who had never existed, of Pentesilia modelled out of nothing, Jean—Racine's Christian name—could, if he felt like it, really mourn for the dead. To enter this domain the authentic heroes of history, whether they were called Alexander or Mithridates, had even to give up what truth there was in them, and throwing off the shroud of history, submit to a classical embalmment. For this cultivated little Christian with his eternal role, born of God and destined for immortality, the symbols of courage, sweetness and friendship, Achilles, Iphigenia or Pollux, were beings whose death was absolute, and whose life was lit by no sacrament. The whole of nature also profited by this privilege. The very "properties" of the world, although they had received Christian baptism, the sun which Joshua had stopped, the stars which had twinkled on the nativity, the flowers and mountains to which Scripture had given a higher life and the power to leap with joy, were authorised to appear for the classical performance in a gilded masquerade, or to imbibe a living soul which would thrust them from that external and fortuitous place which the Church gives them, into the bosom of nature, there to become necessary and formidable organs of her life. It is going a little quickly to say that the schoolmasters thought they would thus develop an intelligence consecrated in the last resort to the service of God. One might just as well affirm that religious establishments encourage gymnastics and sport in order that martyrs should mount the cross blithely or provide the lions of the arena with healthier food. The truth is that for this child, as for so many others before him, his educators favoured the tendency to make the passions a spectacle rather than a reality, to eliminate them by attaching them to illustrious names, in short to repress the outbursts and inconsistencies of the soul by transferring them to celebrated heroes who had never lived, and by enveloping the heart in a firmament of heroes to create a physics and an astronomy of the feelings just as artificial and as useless as real astronomy. All those roles of incest or ambition which Catholicism applauded, Oedipus, Phèdre, Agrippine or Medea, were in a way outlets for the fits of sensitiveness and modesty felt by the Christian brotherhood. They had evidently counted without Racine. They had not foreseen that, faced by two worlds of which the real, wherein he had neither parents nor occupations, was not the less imaginary, this child was bound to choose the one whose passions he could feel and whose life he could make his own. There lies all the realism of Racine, there too the whole history of French realism; for it is likewise the love and respect they had for truth which diverted our great epic and tragic poets from giving France a Valhalla composed of her own citizens. The result has been to leave our heroes outside our culture, to set them in our life and at our level as men. The reality, the finesse, the perfection of human judgment in the French come precisely from the fact that they have never wanted to look at their history and the natural development of their spirit through one of those refracting or coloured lenses which the imagination fixes in the case of other nations. Between Bayard and ourselves, between Charlemagne and ourselves, no trumped up or over-heated atmosphere is allowed to be interposed even through an artifice of genius; canonised kings themselves, like St Louis, remain our contemporaries and command our familiarity. The French nation has given birth to none of those legendary and unreal beings who adorn other civilisations; the middle ages, which furnished Germany with dozens of divine beings, provided us on the contrary with a series of beings astonishingly human. The most fabulous of our national figures are the most real of our heroes, Vercingetorix, Joan of Arc, Napoleon. All those heroes who have emigrated from France to become the mythical personages of other countries, such as William the Conqueror and La Fayette, continue to live in our country a precise, middle-class existence. This impotence or refusal to create legends—so obvious even with the romantics, since the hero of the unique career type when created by German romanticism is called Siegfried and by French romanticism Julien Sorel—ends, as it does in our sculpture, by doubling the human valour and the human aspect of our heroes, giving them, to share between themselves and us, a sort of equality which really makes our country a land of equals. All those Clovises and Pharamonds who with Gaston de Foix and Henry the Great at that time thronged our stage solicited Racine in vain: he withdrew from their appeals precisely because they belonged to his parent stock and not to the stock of his companions, that is, because he did not know them. What gives his heroes and heroines more life than the others have—Corneille's for instance—is that, instead of striking us as being improvised, like the Cid or Polyeucte, they leave the impression of having been long ripened and warmed by the sun of that other world. The life that is in them is in direct ratio to their long absence from our life, and while all other heroes seem to have lived only for a season in the limbo of tragedy, Andromaque, Bérénice and Phèdre have known in their flesh first its spring, then its summer and then its desolation.

Besides, what would Racine have done in a world where pity existed? Under the Catholic religion the really pure sources of misfortune have been pushed back beyond Jesus Christ. Pity, that remorse which is felt by another than the culprit, that rust on good and evil, the one liberty which God has left to men, the only free play accorded them between their start and their goal, is quite the last motive which Racine could admit. What is called his purity comes exactly from the fact that he purified the great sentiments, hatred or love, from this equivocal sentiment. In Racine, the weak or unfortunate characters inspire no pity, nor do the gentle characters feel pity. Like an angel standing with his back to the land of happiness and conciliation, Racine allows none of his creatures to return there, not even for an hour, and as an extra prudence he stiffens their estrangement with stubborn obstinacy. For in all his plays not a single person is convinced by another. Those who hesitate like Roxane or Nero hesitate neither through pity nor reflexion, but through cupidity or hypocrisy. Nor does cowardice exist in them, for cowardice also is a kind of pity on behalf either of oneself or of others. One coward is enough to slacken the tensest drama, and furnishes but a feeble motive at best. Now, contrary to what happens in Corneille, the character in Racine is always more tense than the drama, and the drama does not seem to be, as people have said, the final crisis or paroxysm of the passion of his heroes, but almost their habitual state. It is difficult for us to imagine Polynice, Hermione, Phèdre, Oreste or Athalie in mild or tranquil moments. There were no such moments in their lives. Or at most the drama, instead of being an accident imposed on peaceful and innocent families, on the honest Cid, the brave Horatios, the good Polyeucte, is one of those conflagrations which break out every week in passionate families. All the heroes of Racine form a single frightfully dramatic family before the drama begins. The pitiless storm on Wuthering Heights has more pity in it. The catastrophe is never effected by a solution but by extinction. *Phèdre, Andromaque* and *Bajazet* end because in the first Phèdre and Hippolyte, in the second Hermione and Pyrrhus, in the third Bajazet and Roxane are dead; the *Thébaïde* ends because all are killed, leaving only lay figures on the stage. In Racine's hell the shades of all his heroes find themselves after death with their passions terribly intact and can at once resume their struggle, obstinate as ever though now between shades; whereas one feels that the quarrel between the Cid and Chimène is concluded above to their great satisfaction, and that the Horatios and Curiaces greet one another with outstretched hands. Passion in Racine is vital and incoercible. Hence the joy with which he wrote *Esther* and *Athalie*: he has at last found a fatality more pitiless than the fatality of the ancients, the virulence of which was tempered by the unbelief of the Greeks and the general poetic outlook. He has found his own people. With the Jews he can barter his Greek Destiny for a Jehovah who, beyond the native cruelty of Zeus, has precise designs on mankind. He finds beings who, beside their personal fate, bear in addition a general fatality. He finds the *raison d'être* of such sweet maternal creatures as he calls Josabeth in joyfully watching an old woman, their enemy, die in torment. Lastly he can entrust to a child the role of hatred and cruelty. In this lies the true unity of Racine's plays—that unity which makes the three unities of the Academy useless: in any place, time or phase, the plot would be the same for these characters who have no memories of childhood and innocence, no ordinary adventures common to men, who have never lived in that realm where reconciliation is effected or equality operates, and whose only memories are memories of passion. The ideal summit of tragedy Racine has discovered to be that at which great murders are committed and the darkest souls have complete freedom of movement to perform their highest flights. To this unity in frenzy Racine adds yet another by which all issue in the direction of liberty or ignorance is barred for the characters—unity of blood. All his heroes know one another through and through. While with Corneille or Molière, the stage is the cross-roads which permits or produces chance encounters, for Racine it is either the family sanctuary or the central cage of a menagerie. The heroes rarely meet there by appointment, but there they are thrown together incessantly. A scene in Corneille is an official rendezvous where one comes to discuss in hopes of a settlement. In Racine, it is the explanation which closes for the time a series of negotiations between wild beasts. Nothing was to give a more profound impression of truth to the French, for whom as a nation public tragedies of a romantic sort are on the whole rare, and who keep passion for their domestic quarrels. ...Between Elvire and the Cid, between Camille and her brother, between Polyeucte and his wife there is one settlement to be effected, involving the deepest feelings, and when they part they have said all. The scenes in Racine are as indefinitely renewable as family meals. So little are his people disposed to put an end to them—just as in real families where each one trains and formalises his cruelty by putting it through manœuvres and sharpening its edges daily—that the sign for the finish has to be given from without, not by a decision of one of the characters or the revelation of a psychological truth, but by third-party assassins and by the catastrophe. Love in Racine for instance never provokes a struggle to win a man or a woman in betrothal; it is a debate in the midst of a terrible liaison. And what a liaison! The whole drama of Racine is a drama of incest. That cloud of incest which takes definite shape in Phèdre hovers over all his chief tragedies: Roxane desires her brother-in-law, Mithridate his daughter-in-law twice over, Oreste his cousin. Pyrrhus and Titus each lives with the woman he loves in equivocal promiscuity. Their crimes too are incestuous; Athalie wants to kill her grandson, Agamemnon his daughter, Etéocle and Polynice their brother. Incest alone attracts Racine to Turkey and the seraglio. The characters who simply love partners from whom they are alienated by blood and habitation—Bajazet, Britannicus, Aricie—have not the true Racinian light playing on them and are ready to exchange their bond with Racine for one with Quinault. Racine knows well enough that nothing spreads more quickly in a family than passion, unless it be tuberculosis; and if he exaggerates this dose of family promiscuity it is not only that one should feel all the actors gravitating around the central meeting-place, but because the hero is thus deprived of all resource, all counsel, all solitude. At night a mere partition separates all the heroines of Racine from him they love and from him they abhor—the fiery Pyrrhus from the cold Andromaque. No respite is permitted them, they are goaded perpetually; the same cook feeds them, the same washerwoman looks after their linen, the same noises punctuate their insomnia. All they have to dissimulate their love with are feelings of hatred and scenes of dissension. They have nothing before them but death—not the peaceful return of the *amante* coming back after deceptions or adulteries to a circle which has remained in ignorance or to another home. Once the Racinian hero comes on the stage all the bridges are broken behind him and with his first word he is condemned.

We touch here the clearest point in the art of Racine, the point at which his truth explains itself. Racine's truth does not come from his subjects, nor, as has been said, from the fact that each of them can be reduced to a *fait divers*, for this can be done just as well with Corneille's subjects: the *Cid* is Vendetta, *Polyeucte* is Lourdes. But from the terrible reciprocal knowledge that the heroes of Racine share there results an absolute simplicity of relationship between them. Their characterisation includes nothing that is accessory in thought, deed or costume. They have not to disguise themselves under any false appearance or covering. Never did heroes care so little about their swords, their jewels or their buskins. They mention their veils only to complain of them. Those moral and physical elegances which one guesses belong to the heroes of Corneille and even of Molière, those titivations, those charming, conventionalised "slips" which are distributed to the heroines at the beginning of each love-scene in Goethe and Shakespeare—of all this there is nothing here. In no work of art have the heroes' naked bodies been so distinct from their clothes. The whole wardrobe of Agnès and of Chimène is evoked by their name, the hidden girdle of Desdemona, the pointed neck of Marguerite's dress; while at the name of Andromaque or Iphigénie or Phèdre only their bodies appear; and for his part the spectator, instead of feeling that he wears that kind of adornment which a fine spectacle seems to add to one, feels he has acquired a new skin. From the *Cid* you come away draped, from *Bajazet*, stripped. Completely deprived of inner and outer picturesqueness all the Racinian heroes confront one another on a footing of awful equality, of physical and moral nudity. One cannot help thinking of the equality of tigers; and it is all the more an equality, a verity of the jungle because under this aspect of being creatures of luxury, in this animal nudity of theirs, neither Phèdre nor Hermione has that concern for the spectator which seems to dominate the heroes of Corneille. They are not at ease in his presence and he himself listens only by a supreme indiscretion which Racine gave him the strength to commit. While one breathes relief when the Cid recovers Chimène, a feeling of embarrassment grips you when Phèdre faces Hippolyte or when Roxane clutches Bajazet; then indeed true discretion would consist in departing and leaving them alone.

For beings true in this way and whose speech is never an argument or a mere noise in the throat, not a language was required but a modulation. Let the most negligible distance exist between the subject and the poetry that clothes it, and the truth of Racine is veiled. On this point he was no less real. Since the Pléiade there had subsisted between the thought and its verbal attire a kind of joyously redundant pleura which contained the very humour of the poet. Hardy, Auvray, Corneille, Rotrou are throughout in the centre of their works, not as the romantics are by constructing them out of their memories or aspirations, but by that bombast, that loquacity, that Louis XIII romance quality which fills out the most Roman of their verses with poetical hollows and histrionics. There is nothing similar in Racine. The arching of the chest, the exaggerated manner, that excess of spirits which comes when the creative powers run smoothly, all this is reduced really to a minimum. He has withdrawn from the verse all that was personal to the poet, and of the creative breath not a bubble remains in his works. Never has any creation of human poetry borne so little of a stamp or made so few claims to be the patent of its author or its epoch. None of those arabesques, here, which even God allowed himself when he created gazelles and catfish. Never is the speech of the hero prompted by an author of genius. Never do we get that impression of sublime ventriloquism which, up to Racine's time and ever since, all French tragedians have invariably given us. When images or metaphors occur their effect is prodigious: they are not granules of poetry produced by an inspired mind, but the very speech of a hero, the gleam, the flash, the crepitation caused by the Fabulous coming flush with, dashing its divine body against, our atmosphere. Metaphor is not, as with his forerunners, a flourish of the pen, a poetical challenge, a slight attack of obliviousness to reality, or the full throb and swoon of those singing birds which hear nothing else when they sing; it is the moment when human language changes by reason of the height of the acoustic and the poetic tension into the language of poetry itself. So true is this that Racine's finest metaphors are not reserved for the principal roles, but for supernumeraries, for Pharnace, for confidants or valets. Examination of the vocabulary confirms this statement. Each French word before Racine had a personal, almost a festive life. It was puffed up, as it were, with the pride of an upstart or an adolescent. When it united with others it must do so with curtsies and retreats. All verses written in French before Racine hover round the lips of the poet who wrote them and could be inscribed in one of those streamers which proceed from the mouth of a speaker in a drawing. Racine does not recite, he does not speak his verses. They are all chosen in a dictionary not of beautiful words but of silences. They don't get inside you to form midway between your lips and your heart a goitre of sublimity. None of them presupposes those vocal chords, pharynxes and epiglottises which players of the Hôtel de Bourgogne soothed with *aramon*. They have no false echoes—no true ones either. They make no sign to you, rouse you to no action. Free of equivocal trappings and shady liaisons, the noun, the adjective, and the verb regain their absolute value, and as virgins, mistresses and wives who in other poets give themselves body and soul to the vocabulary, they entrust themselves in Racine only to the syntax. Never did genitives express more delicately and imperiously dependence, or possessives possession, or relatives relation. All Racine's words have, like Racine himself, been withdrawn from the world for twenty years in passionate solitude and chastity, and the meetings effected between the most ordinary terms have a nuptial value and reserve. From this infinitely narrowed distance between expression and the heart there comes at the same time—as if from the pure and dignified language (so similar by the way to Racine's) of children who are being operated on and who awaken under the chloroform—that impression of new life and new truth.

Such is the literary existence of Racine, dominated by so great a poetic fatality that at first glance it may seem moulded by Jansenism—so much do destinies resemble one another when they deserve the name of destiny. Actually his literary existence did not become involved in his human fate until the moment when it handed him over to the latter. The sudden silence of the poet needs no other explanation. His work, free from the age-long anguish of experience, devoid of scruples, morals and reminiscences, breaks down at a certain moment—not when the author ascends to virtue or aspires to some superior order of ideas—but simply when he enters life. Once that portion of the unconscious indispensable for Racine to achieve his dual function of archangel and executioner had melted away, the cruelty and virginity which had characterised his literary existence had no more chance to superimpose themselves upon his suddenly constituted bourgeois life with its royal charge, moral judgment, wife and children conceived and bred in piety. The reason why he stopped writing is this: that one fine day he ceased to be a writer. Why not because he had nothing more to say? some ask. It would have been the first time a writer had stopped for such a motive. On the contrary it was because the knowledge of life came to him in its most banal and pathetic forms, with children, a king, a tumour, with the emotions and struggles that the functions of a courtier and a moral being involve, and sometimes even under the aspect of a genre which had no vogue at that time on the stage, namely drama. In the life of each of us the deeds that are tragic do not always correspond to the critical moment of our destiny. Never has this divergence been pushed farther than in the life of our greatest tragic poet. If Racine becomes silent after *Phèdre*, it is not because *Phèdre* was by its nature the last of his pieces. It was on the contrary the first of what would have been a series of terrific plays; and the misfortune for us is that the poet only felt himself completely let loose at the precise moment when a coalition of prejudices, friends, enemies, duties and responsibilities fixed their bonds upon the man. He revealed himself as at once the stage-manager of a world of terrors and the servant of a court. Racine's tragedy was beginning, and like the tragedy of all his plays, it could only finish with someone's death, that of the poet himself. It was not silence but suicide. It cannot be said that during the finest fifteen years of the great century the greatest French poet held his peace. He did not hold his peace, he no longer existed. We know what a poet's silence is like, we guess its nuances and the constant pleasure it must provide. Racine's silence was that of a stone. It was not gossiping with oneself like the silence of La Fontaine; it was not swollen with echoes, with rhymes, with contradictions of mood having the beauty of successful enjambments, or with the perfect plenitude of distiches whose two verses have been conceived at the same moment. Serene and deaf to appeals, it was a constant refusal to condense the atmosphere into its poetic precipitate. Whereas with La Fontaine or Vigny, for their silence to change suddenly into harmony, it sufficed to give physical consent to the impulses of brain and blood, to break the silence of Racine required a judgment, a moral decision which henceforth he would not deign to make. The granulation of the soul into hexameters no longer operated. The purest French ever written was no longer for Racine the perfect language, but the dialect of a country he had abandoned. Those spiritual trances which used to throw a mist over the aspects of seventeenth-century Paris and re-shape them after the antique had yielded to frigidity. Not only Racine but all the Racinian voices were hushed—hushed for Racine alone in the world he had created. Even the Racinian style has become foreign to him, he has forgotten it: in *Athalie* he employs whole hexameters from *Andromaque* or other pieces. So little of himself has he re-read for ten years. Changed into a hard man in the midst of a universe transformed into a world of insensibility, he is mute and his muteness—it is not surprising—is absolute. For this man now married—more attracted by the sacrament than by the marriage—there is a degree of illegitimacy about conception and paternity in the literary sense which is intolerable and makes him blush. He does not like to hear his legitimate children, whose number by the way is exactly that of the tragedies of his happy period, speak to him of their bastard sisters. One has the impression that he has likewise surrendered to the vicissitudes of a banal and changing life that form of woman he had meant to confine exclusively to an endless youth, and that for those heroines whom he had fixed immovable in their splendour, he reopens in imagination the highway to death, he alone of all people seeing Andromaque with grey hair and then with white, Roxane puffed and wrinkled, Phèdre ataxic. In him alone that form which no age has touched begins to grow old and becomes Athalie. That old wench there, that is what Hermione and Bérénice have become for the sole reason that life having at last touched Racine, death touches what he had created. For the world of imagination which we have depicted he has the hardness which the responsibility of life gives, and a certain hatred. It is wrong to say that his Catholic conscience diverted him from writing. It would soon have commanded him to write. It is the duty of every Christian to use the gifts which God has given him, and Racine did not hide from himself that he possessed some of the writer's talents. What God forbids is the doubter's game of staking at the same time on literature and on God. He forbids the writer to hold an inferior view of literature and to try to ennoble and justify it by slipping religion in underhand or to graft his literary nervous system on the divine. God likes literature to be literary and nothing else, just as the only philosophy he likes is the theoretical. Racine had therefore every right, and was right in his own eyes, either to continue to work in that state of unconsciousness about Christianity which dispels all mists round the writer and sets him in a pure atmosphere which is not disagreeable to look down on from above, or by using his talent in the praise of God, to devote himself to that divine journalism which produced, along with a few great poets, the prophets and the greater prelates. No, Racine is silent because he is no longer a writer; and to make him speak again, it is obvious that, since the affection and those imaginary passions which had formerly inspired him are decayed, one real passion at least is required, and the object of this passion must appeal to his former talent. Fortunately for us this is what happened. It turned out that Racine experienced the only passion that can fall upon the soul of a bourgeois in its hard, deliberate narrowness. He loves the king. He loves him in his person and in his essence. That delegation of authority which God grants to kings permits each Christian soul to exercise, not only with impunity but even with nobility, all the pagan idolatry that the soul contains. A king is the idol authorised by God; upon him God diverts the feelings which, pushed to extremes, are incompatible both with humanity and with the creator: devotion, affection, physical submission. Between love of God and love of the sovereign there are none of those rivalries which the other passions present. God declines affection; even to-day in the most democratic realms what is felt for the king and the heir to the throne by railway guards and barristers is affection. Given a king, the heart is no longer alone. You lift your king up and put him to bed like the doll you love. His smile, his good temper brighten the day like omens. Racine's education and his tastes prepared him for this role of pagan priest. For him more than for anyone, the simplest words of the king, the frown or the gaiety of the king seemed to come from the source of all smiles, anger and argument, and simply to connect words and gestures with their divine prototype. Privileged by nature, which had given him at birth that resemblance to the monarch which the bourgeois obtain only after years of daily application, he considered that visage, his own face deified, as what was most different from himself and farthest removed: he loved it with all that love involves, torment, delight and death. This explains *Esther* and *Athalie*, and the sudden appearance of the two poems in the midst of this insensibility. From the isle where they had been prisoners for ten years, one fine day all the Racinian amazons disembarked to land at the abode of Virgins. Destiny, after having imposed a brutal separation, has no compunction in allowing great souls to return to their great tasks for a few weeks, drawn together for the last time by a supreme lure before exile and cancer supervene.

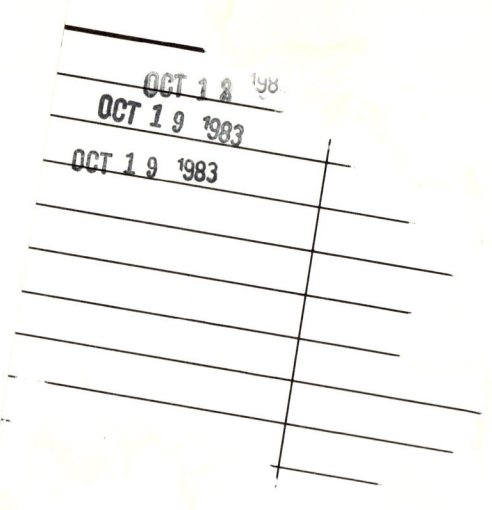